The Pizza Patch

Jill McDougall

OXFORD
UNIVERSITY PRESS

OXFORD
UNIVERSITY PRESS

Great Clarendon Street, Oxford, OX2 6DP, United Kingdom

Oxford University Press is a department of the University
of Oxford. It furthers the University's objective of excellence
in research, scholarship, and education by publishing
worldwide. Oxford is a registered trade mark of Oxford
University Press in the UK and in certain other countries

Text © Jill McDougall 2014

The moral rights of the author have been asserted

First published 2014

All rights reserved. No part of this publication may
be reproduced, stored in a retrieval system, or transmitted,
in any form or by any means, without the prior permission in
writing of Oxford University Press, or as expressly permitted
by law, by licence or under terms agreed with the appropriate
reprographics rights organization. Enquiries concerning
reproduction outside the scope of the above should be sent to the
Rights Department, Oxford University Press, at the address above.

You must not circulate this work in any other form
and you must impose this same condition on any acquirer

British Library Cataloguing in Publication Data
Data available

ISBN: 978-0-19-830810-2

10 9 8 7 6 5 4 3 2 1

Paper used in the production of this book is a natural, recyclable product
made from wood grown in sustainable forests. The manufacturing process
conforms to the environmental regulations of the country of origin.

Printed in China by Hing Yip

Acknowledgements

Series Editor: Nikki Gamble
Illustrations by Agnese Baruzzi
Photography by Lindsay Edwards

The publishers would like to thank the following for the permission to
reproduce photographs: Cover photos by Primopiano/Shutterstock; Vitaly
Korovin/Shutterstock; Diana Taliun/Shutterstock; Improvize/Shutterstock;
Natasha Breen/Shutterstock; Jessmine/Shutterstock. Background images
by Aksenenko Olga/Shutterstock; Primopiano/Shutterstock; Chieferu/
iStockphoto; Elena Kalistratova/Shutterstock; Picsfive/Shutterstock; Tratong/
Shutterstock; Brandon Bourdages/Shutterstock; DenisNata/Shutterstock;
Johann Helgason/Shutterstock.

Contents

- The Best Spot — 4
- Watch Out, Weeds! — 6
- The Pizza Patch — 8
- A Lot of Rot — 10
- From Flower to Fruit — 12
- The Worm Farm — 14
- Pesky Pests — 16
- The Scarecrow — 18
- Time to Pick! — 20
- The Pizza Party — 22
- Glossary and Index — 24

The Best Spot

by CHARLOTTE

Today is cool and cloudy.

We're going to build a food garden at school. Today, Mrs Lee helped us to plan it.

This spot looks good!

First, we found the best place for our garden. It's a sunny spot that's sheltered from the wind. It's close to a water tap, and Mrs Lee says it has really good soil, too.

Mrs Lee knows everything about gardening.

If we plan our garden well, hopefully we will grow lots of food.

OUR GARDEN PLAN

- garden beds
- fruit trees
- compost bins
- worm farm
- chicken coop

Watch Out, Weeds!

by KEVIN

Today is hot and windy.

Today, everyone helped build the garden. Gemma and I dug up **weeds** and put them in a bucket of water. In a few weeks, we will take the rotting weeds out of the water and put them in the **compost** bin.

Watch out, weeds!

We don't stand a chance!

Our new garden is ready for planting!

The Pizza Patch

by STELLA

Today is bright and sunny.

Today, we made a pizza patch – we really did! A pizza patch grows vegetables and herbs to go on pizzas.

TIPS FOR MAKING A PIZZA PATCH

1. Pull the weeds out of your garden bed and rake the soil.

2. Add some **manure**.

3. Add some straw to keep the soil from getting dry.

4. Plant different **seedlings** in different parts of the garden bed. Each plant will grow a topping for a pizza.

We are growing tomatoes, spring onions, courgettes and basil for our pizzas.

Josh and I are planting a tomato seedling.

A Lot of Rot

by ZOE

Today is hot and dry.

Today, we made compost. Compost is made from lots of things that rot. It's a great **fertilizer** for plants.

Emily and I are putting some leaves into the compost bin.

COMPOST RECIPE

You will need:

- green stuff (fresh grass and plant clippings)

- brown stuff (dried leaves and straw)

- fruit and vegetable scraps

- a handful of soil

- water.

What to do:

- Put the green stuff, brown stuff, scraps and soil into your compost bin.

- Then sprinkle on some water until the pile is damp.

- Over time, everything will rot and ... guess what! You've made compost!

From Flower to Fruit

by <u>ALEX</u>

Today is warm.

Big yellow flowers are growing on the <u>courgette</u> plant. Behind them, baby courgettes are starting to <u>grow</u>!

1 Flowers grow on the plant.

2 Bees move **pollen** from one flower to another.

3 Tiny courgettes start to grow.

13

The Worm Farm

by MARCUS

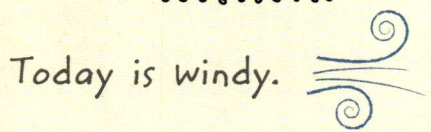

Today is windy.

Today, we looked at our worm farm. The worms munch on food scraps and leave behind heaps of worm poo (called castings).

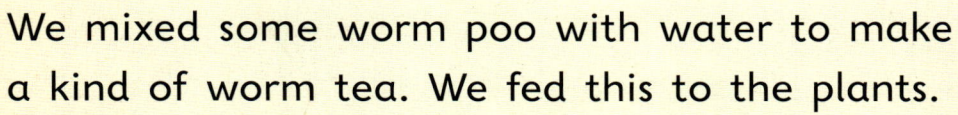

We mixed some worm poo with water to make a kind of worm tea. We fed this to the plants.

Worms are cool.

Our worm tea will help the plants grow.

Eww, worm poo!

THE WORM FARM

Chomp! Chomp!

straw

food scraps

lots of worms

worm castings

TODAY'S MENU

teabags

apple cores

eggshells

water that drips out

15

Pesky Pests

by VANESSA

Today is showery.

Help! The pizza patch is being invaded! It's not aliens invading our garden, it's pests. Snails are snacking on the basil and slugs are chomping on the tomatoes.

We picked off the pests and fed them to the chickens.

Gulp!

GOT YOU!

We catch snails and slugs with old orange halves. They creep under them to hide from the sun.

BUGS THAT EAT OTHER BUGS

Not all bugs in the garden are pests. These bugs feed on the pesky plant-eaters.

ladybird

lacewing

hoverfly

ground beetle

The Scarecrow

by ANDY

Today is sunny.

Some of the cherry tomatoes are ripe. I popped one in my mouth and splat — it burst open! It was warm and sweet — yum!

Birds like to eat tomatoes, too. We had to come up with a plan to scare them away, so we made a **scarecrow!**

Yikes!

Scarecrows can keep birds away.

Time to Pick!

by <u>GEORGE</u>

Today is warm.

Hooray – the pizza plants are ready for picking! Tomorrow we'll have a pizza party!

Today we picked:

- tomatoes
- courgettes
- basil leaves
- spring onions.

The Pizza Party

by CHARLOTTE

Today is bright and sunny.

Today the school kitchen was a busy place. We made pizza dough and chopped up our vegetables. Soon we could smell the pizzas cooking!

My pizza had cheese, courgette, tomato, basil and spring onion on it. I was about to pick up a slice when ... oops! A hungry caterpillar had crawled onto my pizza!

Glossary

compost: a mixture of rotten plants and rotten food that is used to feed living plants

fertilizer: food for plants

manure: poo from animals such as cows, horses and chickens

pollen: a powder found inside flowers

scarecrow: something that looks like a person and is used to scare birds away

seedlings: young plants grown from seed

weeds: plants that grow where you don't want them to grow

Index

basil	9, 16, 21, 23
cheese	23
chickens	5, 16
compost	5, 6, 10–11
courgettes	9, 12, 21, 23
kitchen	22
pests	16–17
pizza	8–9, 20, 22–23
scarecrow	18–19
spring onions	9, 21, 23
tomatoes	9, 16, 18–19, 21, 23
weeds	6–7, 8
worms	14–15